THE INSIDE JOURNEY

Poems from the Heart

BY TRACY LOCKLEAR

Copyright 2019 Tracy Locklear
All rights reserved and in compliance under the United States of America Copyright Law. No part or portion of this book can be used or reproduced by any means, without the written consent of the author as the publisher.

Book Preparation and Production services by Pillar Publishing & Company, LLC. Richmond, VA
www.pillarpublishingcompany.org
Pillar Publishing & Company is not responsible for any content of the book.

Book edited by Sharon Arredondo

       ISBN: 97800-578-50543-5

Contents

DEDICATION	
WINTER	1
PEOPLE	3
TRUST	5
WALLS	7
DREAMS	9
A VOICE	10
A TOUCH	13
THE SWEETEST THING	15
ONE FINE DAY	17
A CRYING HEART	19
WHO DO YOU SEE?	21
RANDOM THOUGHTS	23
LOST IN YOU	25
CAPTIVE	27
FRIENDS	29
GRANDPARENTS	31
MY GIRLS	33

Dedication

This book is dedicated to my beautiful daughters, T'keyah and Chanell. I am so proud of both of you. You are my greatest joy and gifts from God. I love you so much.

Winter

The time of year when it's cold outside,
When you have to take everything in stride.

The time of year when the snow falls deep,
When you're driving so slowly, it's almost at a creep.

The time of year when you dread getting out of bed,
When it's cold inside and you have to cover everything even your head.

The time of year when long johns are worn to keep warm,
When you have to work even when they call for a winter storm.

The time of year to build snowmen and make snow angels,
When you decorate a tree and sing jingle bells.

The time of year for kids and adults to have snowball fights,
When you go skiing even though you are afraid of heights.

The time of year to share and exchange gifts,
When you are feeling down this will give you a lift.

The time of year for love happiness and joy,
When your average truck driver is no longer a boy.

People

There are a lot of people in this world;
Some of them nice, some of them mean
Short-haired, long-haired, straight-haired and curled
All shapes and sizes the most popular lean.

I've met a lot of people not all of them nice
First and last impressions make you think twice.
But it's the in between that makes you who you are
That's why I think of you all as a shining star.

Trust

At first, I gave it all to you without a doubt;
without a question, because we were new.

As time went on you chipped away at it like wood.
Damn, can you just do the things you said you could?

Building me up to tear me down was a mistrust of my feelings ...
I almost drowned.

I trusted you with my body that was my mistake
You treated it like it was your property, your whipping post, who knew it could hate.

I trusted you with my mind so delicate and true
You felt the need to put on your mean word boots and stomp your way through.

My heart was completely destroyed, all because you were annoyed.
I thought I could give it to you freely.
I WAS WRONG!!!

Walls

The walls are closing in, I can't seem to breathe
Front, back, side to side, I run but can't leave.

Life sometimes is good to you, so sweet and nice
But other times it cuts deep, deep like a knife.

Walls are everywhere like leaves on trees
They keep you safe inside, kind of binding like cheese.

At times, I want to hit them, even knock them down
Just to not feel like I'm going to drown.

Sometimes, I wish I had doors on the walls of my brain
So, I could slam shut the doors on my thoughts of pain.

Such a rush of thoughts like rain break through
You have to grab some meds, maybe a zane or two.

Walls are built for shelter, to divide, and for protection
For memories, secrets, wrong doing and decoration.

Walls are designed to do many things.
I can't wait to be free and take flight with my wings.

Dreams

Sometimes I dream while I'm asleep
They make me laugh, they make me weep.

Some dreams scour the surface
While others go very, very deep.

Some dreams seem so real
They get inside where you feel.

You can't control them, you can't get away
Some so frightening that words can't say.

I dream a dream of beautiful waters
That take you to places you can't imagine really matters.

It's a place filled with warmth, love, and nothing mean
I guess that's why this place exists only in my dreams.

A Voice

There came a day when I finally noticed.

Such a sweet and simple thing.
A very gentle, pleasing sound on the other end of a ring.

A sound like soft music after a hard day of work
A sound if you don't hear for a while, will make you go berserk.

It's a common thing that everyone shares
That mostly goes unnoticed as if no one cares.

A sound even when irritated, doesn't take it out on you
And does not make you feel bad when you're sad and blue.

I can't help but wonder who holds such a beautiful thing?
So, I'll sit and wait and see what tomorrow will bring.

Hopefully, one day I'll get the choice
Of when I get to meet the person who holds that very sweet voice.

A Touch

Something you feel when someone's close to you.

Something you can count on to always to be true.

It sometimes sends goose bumps up and down your spine.
It's something you long for when you've had too much wine

It's something that feels so soft, gentle, and warm;
You could wrap yourself in it and get lost in its charm.

A simple thing that expresses a lot and if done correctly, may even get you hot.

When you're close enough to someone to kiss their lips
You should get a tingling feeling that runs to your hips.

It's something that should not cause you pain
It should not be a feeling like hail in rain.

It should always be kind, sweet, and loving
It would also be nice if it included some hugging.

The Sweetest Thing

The sweetest thing to me is someone being nice for no reason
A person willing to help you no matter what the season.

When you look into someone's eyes and see kindness in their heart
That's the kind of person you want near and not apart.

A person whose words warm you on the inside
Kind of like watching a sunset roll in off a tide.

It's a kindness that shines through with no effort at all
That's what you have and why you stand so tall.

One Fine Day

One fine September day, while walking through the park with nothing to say;
I gazed into your eyes in that very special way
You smiled at me and I smiled at you
It was like seeing dolphins swim in the deep blue.

With every breath you took
It was like all my insides shook.

You bring out the best in me
You make me feel special and free.

Being with you is such a sweet blessing
Like having turkey and cornbread dressing.

You gently caress my face and pull me near
So close with every heartbeat I hear.

You slowly lean in and kiss my lips
So strong, yet soft, it was felt in my hips.

Alone in the park still nothing was said
It was like angels were flying overhead.

One fine day!

A Crying Heart

When you needed me the most, I wasn't there
I feel so helpless, hurt, and empty inside much like a cupboard bare.

You were afraid and alone, no one to help you
The thought alone that I wasn't there for you is worse than anything times two.

You were but a child with no one to protect you, and put your mind at ease
I'm your mother, it's been 23 years and sometimes I still can't breathe.

My heart bleeds with your silence
Because I know what happened was violence.

Your pain is my pain;
On my heart is a permanent stain.
God please help me to find a way
To put the pain away to stay.

Until then, for however many years
I'll continue to be broken hearted and cry tears.

My heart will forever be buried 6 feet
From what you suffered alone in those sheets.

Who Do You See?

Who do you see when you look at me?
Is it Tracy, or the girl you want me to be?
Do you want to know the person you see?
Or am I someone you're with because your time is free?
Am I someone you see that you can control?

Weak and soft spoken, you can't have my soul!

I'm not someone you can use at will
To do as you say, then crush like a pill.

You are not supposed to treat me like your child
You don't hit me when I'm late from work ... for that you're wild.

Do you see me as someone beneath you?
Someone you can step on with your shoe?
Someone you can cheat on as if my feelings don't matter?
I HATE YOU! It replays in my mind like chit chatter.

I don't deserve to be treated this way
Wait! Maybe you never really wanted me to stay.

My heart is crying without a doubt
Come in and save me, stop shutting me out.

Random Thoughts

Thoughts of sadness fill the air
As I realize no one really cares.

I don't have this feeling often
I hate the way this makes my heart soften

Thoughts of caring for someone is frightening;
Almost, as terrifying as being struck by lightning
I never knew I could be so afraid
Of a feeling that is so naturally made.

Thoughts of comfort takes worries away;
Something I hope to do one day
To be a friend is a special thing
Like an early morning when birds sing.

Thoughts of laughter and seeing you smile;
Fills my heart with joy all the while
Talking to you is so relaxing
Unlike the government who is always taxing.

Thoughts of happiness that don't go away;
A field of butterflies on a sunny day
A beautiful waterfall off a mountain top
The calming sound of every raindrop.

Thoughts of a soft warm kiss;
A feeling in your bones, something so intense
A cool breeze on your face on a hot day
Then realize nothing is going your way.

I often visit a dream world with my heart
Then reality sets in, that's why I have random thoughts.

Lost In You

I have felt these words like a weight in my chest;
Tossing and turning, I can't get any rest
I am amazed my heart can go on beating under such pressure
Realizing that it's the aggressor.

I love you, I love you desperately, violently, tenderly, completely and unconditionally
I give you all of me faithfully.

I want you in ways I myself find shocking
So much so my own body starts reacting.

I want to kiss every inch of you, make you hot, sweaty and tremble in ecstasy
So, you can feel what I feel when you stand next to me.

If you only knew how I crave the taste of you;
I want to take you in my hands and mouth and feast on you.
I want to drink all of you in
Like fancy imported gin...

I can't stop thinking about you
Thoughts come in and stick like glue.

Your hands all over my body, your mouth open for my kisses
It's like a dream come true plus my wishes.

I need too much of you, like a drug you have me in cuffs;
A lifetime of nights spent with you inside me wouldn't be enough.

Captive

I want to talk and laugh with you forever, remember every word you say to me.

If I could visit you as if I was a foreigner visiting a new country, learn the language of you, wander past all borders into your secret places,
I would stay forever, I would become a citizen of you.

You may ask how I could be so certain this soon, but somethings can't be measured by time.
Ask me an hour from now, a month, a year, a lifetime from now,
the way I love you will outlast every calendar, clock, every ray of sunshine.

You're my first thought in morning and my last thought before I fall asleep
and you're almost every thought in between.

I can't imagine my life without you;
my love for you runs so deep the ocean is jealous.

It's so natural to feel how I do about you ...
you have a very special place in my heart.

My thoughts are your thoughts, your ways are not my ways
but our love is so strong because we fit in so many other ways.

You're my cave to hide in, my cliff to climb.

Be my safe leader, my true mountain guide, free me from hidden traps,
I want to hide in you.

Friends

I first met you years ago
Nothing special, we said hello.

As time passed, we talked a little more
The talks we had made my heart less sore.

What I found in you is not easy to find
Someone who puts the needs of others before their own, too kind.

You slipped into a place I wasn't prepared for you to be
Damn it boy, you're supposed to be free.

Like ships passing in the night
My feelings should take flight for the sake of what's right.

I want to be your sky, so blue and high
That every time you think of me, I will blow your mind.
Or, I can be your air, so sweet and fair
And in those moments you feel you can't breathe, I'll be there.

This is where we are now as friends
I pray we always have it and it never ends.

I've put my heart in your hands, you won't drop it, and you won't let me down.

Grandparents

Grandparents are a blessing from God
Because most times they don't spank or use a rod.

They spoil you rotten from the time of birth
They look into your eyes like you're the best thing on earth.

Grandparents care for you when your parents can't
They love and nurture you and wash out your pants.

They take you outside and read you books
They keep you safe from harm and dirty crooks.

Grandparents teach you right from wrong
And at bedtime may even sing you a song,

They wake in the middle of the night
When you seem to be in such a fright.

Grandparents rub and hug all your pains away
Then give you cookies and send you off to play.

They take you to church on Sunday to pray
In hopes the little angel they see will stay.

Grandparents give you the best gifts
Full of love, tender thoughts and without having fits.

When it's cold outside, they keep you warm every time,
And when they take you to the store, will spend their very last dime.

Grandparents are the best at giving support
And when the world seems tough, their arms are like a fort.

They love you unconditionally and that's a fact;
I know because I wish I had my grandparents back.

My Girls

My girls, they mean the world to me
As their mom I'm the happiest I can be.

They have grown into beautiful young ladies
Despite all of the hardships they encountered as babies.

My oldest, so strong, independent and full of love
Her smile is so sweet, it's warming like a glove.

My youngest, so bright, so good with children
She has a heart of gold, hands that care, eyes that speak deep within.

I was blessed with two wonderful girls, great moms now
They love me unconditionally, still blows my mind, wow!

To have given birth to them was my greatest joy
Now, I have four grandchildren, the best feeling – all boys.

Growing up, I never really wanted any children of my own
Apparently, God knew I would need their love, to fill the emptiness of feeling alone.

www.ingramcontent.com/pod-product-compliance
Lightning Source LLC
Chambersburg PA
CBHW021413290426
44108CB00010B/513